weird but true! 7

NATIONAL
GEOGRAPHIC
KiDS

weird but true! 7

350 OUTRAGEOUS FACTS

NATIONAL GEOGRAPHIC
WASHINGTON, D.C.

On average, the **Empire State Building** in New York City is hit by **lightning** 25 times a year.

AN ITALIAN DESIGNER MADE A **COUCH** SHAPED LIKE A **CHOCOLATE BAR.**

RED-FOOTED TORTOISES HAVE BEEN TAUGHT TO USE TOUCH **SCREENS.**

Sitting in a **cardboard box** can lower **stress** for **domestic cats.**

Your brain makes up only **2 percent** of your total body weight but uses up to **20 percent** of your body's energy.

HONEYBEES HAVE **TWO** STOMACHS.

Some **frogs** have **green bones.**

A **house** in England was built out of **20,000** used toothbrushes, **two tons** of old jeans, (1.8 t) **4,000** DVD cases, and other waste items.

GOLDEN
ORB-WEAVING
SPIDERS
THAT LIVE IN
CITIES
GROW BIGGER
THAN ONES IN
RURAL AREAS.

SARCASTIC
FRINGEHEAD FISH
BATTLE
OVER TURF BY
WRESTLING
EACH OTHER WITH
THEIR MOUTHS.

THE HEAVIEST **CAULIFLOWER** ON RECORD WEIGHED MORE **THAN A BULLDOG.**

UP TO HALF OF THE WATER ON EARTH IS OLDER THAN THE SUN, ACCORDING TO ONE STUDY.

Earwax is a natural antibiotic.

DON'T TRY TO USE THE STICKY STUFF AS MEDICINE!

Food travels through your esophagus at a speed of about one inch (2.5 cm) a second.

3,000,000,000

MORE THAN THREE BILLION PASSENGERS TRAVEL ON COMMERCIAL AIRPLANES EVERY YEAR.

A STUDY FOUND THAT **CHEWING GUM** PUTS YOU IN A **BETTER MOOD.**

ONE MAN INVENTED **A SUPERFAST POTATO PEELER** OUT OF A TOILET BRUSH ATTACHED TO A DRILL.

A SPANISH SCIENTIST INVENTED **ICE CREAM** THAT **CHANGES COLORS** WHEN **LICKED.**

THE **PUDU**—
A SMALL
KIND OF DEER—
RUNS IN A
ZIGZAG
PATTERN
TO ESCAPE
PREDATORS.

YOU HAVE TASTE RECEPTORS IN YOUR STOMACH.

SPITTING SPIDERS IMMOBILIZE PREY BY SPRAYING THEM WITH POISONOUS

It takes more than **ten** gallons (38 L) of **water** to make one **slice of bread.**

The average wait time at a **fast-food** restaurant drive-through is **232 seconds.**

SPECIAL VENDING MACHINES IN ISTANBUL, TURKEY, AUTOMATICALLY DISPENSE FOOD AND WATER FOR DOGS.

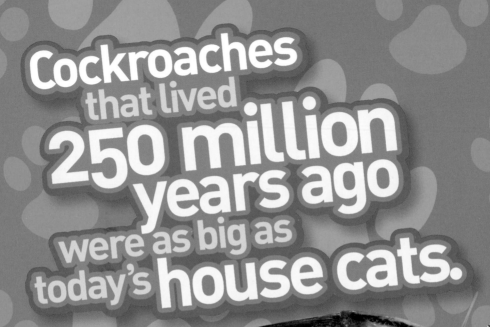

Cockroaches that lived **250 million** years ago were as big as today's **house cats.**

23

ARTIST CHARLES M. SCHULZ CREATED NEARLY 18,000 "PEANUTS" COMIC STRIPS.

Scientists have found a way to return hard-boiled egg whites to liquid form.

Some airplane pilots use a beach on Fraser Island, Australia, as a landing strip.

PASSENGERS ARRIVING AT ONE
NEW ZEALAND AIRPORT ARE GREETED BY A
14-FOOT BUST OF THE **DRAGON**
(4.3-m)
Smaug **FROM *THE HOBBIT***
MOVIE TRILOGY.

Scientists think that the center of the moon may be SQUISHY.

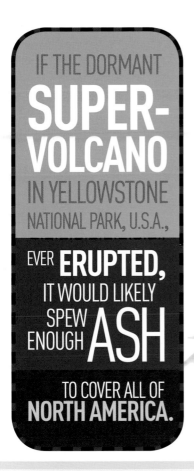

IF THE DORMANT **SUPER-VOLCANO** IN YELLOWSTONE NATIONAL PARK, U.S.A., EVER **ERUPTED,** IT WOULD LIKELY SPEW ENOUGH **ASH** TO COVER ALL OF **NORTH AMERICA.**

The **Pac-Man frog** can lift three times its own **body weight** with its tongue.

LISTENING TO **CLASSICAL MUSIC** CAN HELP **DOGS RELAX,** A STUDY FOUND.

A DUTCH COMPANY PLANS TO BUILD A **SNOWFLAKE-SHAPED HOTEL** THAT FLOATS ON **WATER.**

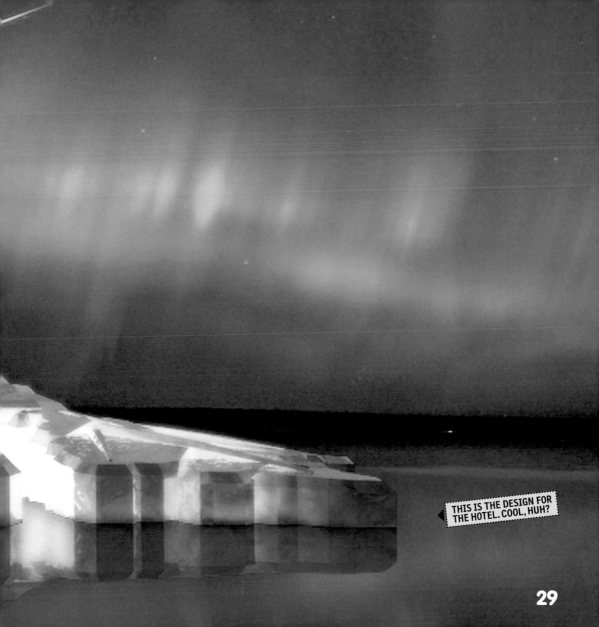

THIS IS THE DESIGN FOR THE HOTEL. COOL, HUH?

29

A NEWSPAPER IN SRI LANKA

was printed with insect-repelling ink to keep readers from getting bug bites.

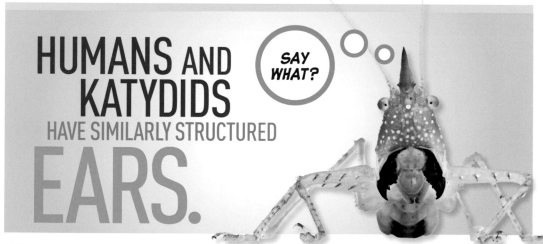

HUMANS AND KATYDIDS
HAVE SIMILARLY STRUCTURED
EARS.

SAY WHAT?

THE GIANT **PITCHER PLANT** SECRETES **NECTAR** TO LURE BUGS AND RODENTS INTO ITS "**MOUTH.**"

A SOUTH KOREAN BASEBALL TEAM INSTALLED

CHEERING ROBOTS

IN THE STANDS OF ITS BALLPARK.

A record **232 people** did a **cannonball dive** all at once into a harbor in New Zealand.

ONE KIND OF **MUSHROOM** RESEMBLES A **HUMAN BRAIN.**

Between 1886 and 1902, the *Statue of Liberty* was used as a lighthouse.

Humans may have once had a third eyelid.

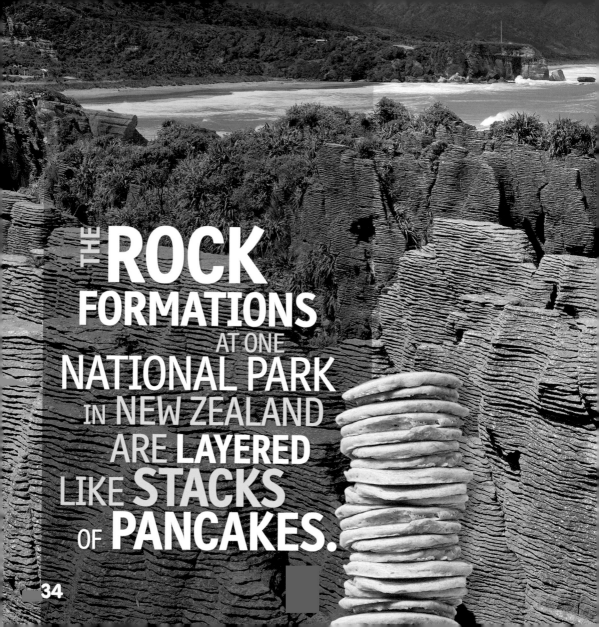

THE **ROCK** **FORMATIONS** AT ONE NATIONAL PARK IN NEW ZEALAND ARE **LAYERED** LIKE **STACKS** OF **PANCAKES.**

GIANT CUTTLEFISH HAVE BAGEL-SHAPED BRAINS.

During the **Ice Age, supersize Lions roamed** what is now the United Kingdom.

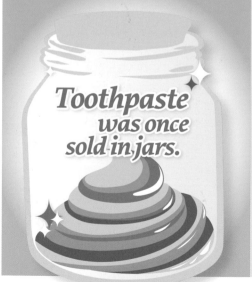

Toothpaste was once sold in jars.

HUMMINGBIRDS FLAP THEIR WINGS UP TO 80 TIMES A SECOND.

IT WOULD TAKE A SPACESHIP ABOUT 450 MILLION YEARS TO REACH THE EDGE OF OUR GALAXY.

A **HIKER** IN COLORADO, U.S.A., SCARED OFF A **MOUNTAIN LION** THAT WAS **STALKING HER** BY SINGING **OPERA.**

A KIND OF **BIRD** THAT LIVED 25 MILLION YEARS AGO HAD A **WINGSPAN** LONGER THAN SIX BASEBALL **BATS.**

SOME RAINBOWS APPEAR TO

CONTAIN ONLY SHADES OF RED.

About **400 hours** of new videos are posted to **YouTube** every minute.

You don't **sneeze** while you're sleeping.

ONE **WOMAN WALKED 10,000 MILES** (16,093 km) **ACROSS ASIA AND AUSTRALIA IN THREE YEARS.**

SPUTNIK 1, THE FIRST SATELLITE IN SPACE, WAS ABOUT THE SIZE OF A BEACH BALL.

Hundreds of years ago, it was common for people in Naples, Italy, **TO EAT PASTA WITH THEIR BARE HANDS.**

Some **BIRDS** eat **BEESWAX.**

In Spanish-speaking countries, the toxic manchineel tree is known as the **"TREE OF DEATH."**

The **TIANJIN EYE**, a Ferris wheel in **CHINA**, is suspended over the **Hai River.**

Thousands of bacteria live on just one **STRAND** of your **HAIR.**

An unmanned **AIR FORCE** plane spent **718** DAYS **ORBITING EARTH.**

March 6 is **NATIONAL OREO DAY** in the United States.

A man in the United Kingdom **TRAINED** his cocker spaniel to **RESCUE LOST CATS.**

Deep-sea creatures called **LARVACEANS** create **"HOUSES"** OUT OF THEIR SNOT.

A chef in New York City created a savory doughnut made out of spaghetti.

The EXOPLANET **KELT-11b** is 40 PERCENT LARGER than JUPITER but is about as DENSE AS STYROFOAM.

THE WALNUT SPHINX CATERPILLAR makes a whistling sound TO SCARE OFF HUNGRY BIRDS.

A SHORTFIN MAKO SHARK traveled more than **11,600** miles (18,670 km) in one year—**that's** almost **halfway** around the world.

That's Weird!

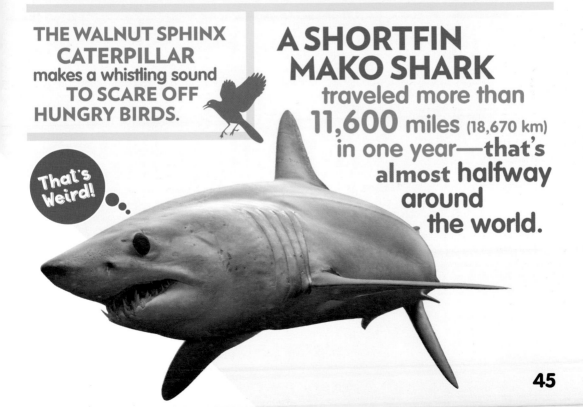

At an annual race in Totnes, England, competitors kick oranges along the course as they run.

On average, a **$1 bill** is in **circulation** in the United States for about **six years.**

The first **item sold on eBay was a broken laser pointer.**

A **cobra** bit a chef in China **20** minutes

AFTER its head had been CUT from its body.

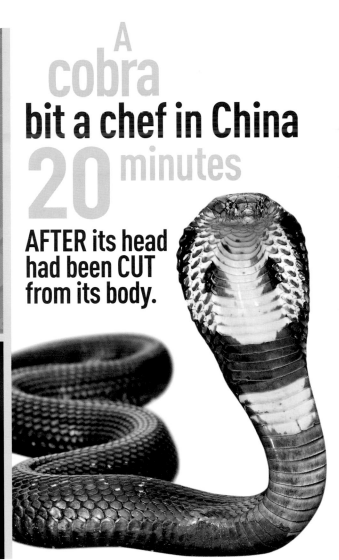

47

EACH YEAR, WINDS BLOW ABOUT 40 MILLION TONS OF DUST (36 million t) FROM AFRICA'S SAHARA ...

TO THE
AMAZON RIVER BASIN
IN SOUTH AMERICA.

There are more than 20,000 TV stations in the world.

FOUND IN
AUSTRALIA AND
NEW GUINEA, THE
**SOUTHERN
CASSOWARY
BIRD**
HAS CLAWS NEARLY
THE LENGTH
OF AN iPHONE.

The **coati,** a member of the raccoon family, can rotate its ankles **180 degrees.**

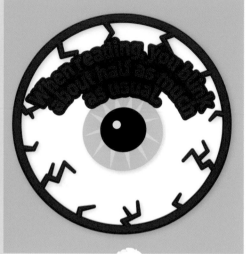

When reading, you blink about half as much as usual.

MORE THAN **29,000** GRAINS ARE IN A ONE-POUND (0.5-kg) BAG OF RICE.

A **HEXAGON-SHAPED HURRICANE** HAS HOVERED OVER SATURN'S NORTH POLE FOR AT LEAST **30 YEARS.**

SCIENTISTS THINK OUR SUN HAS A "SIBLING"— A STAR 110 LIGHT-YEARS AWAY

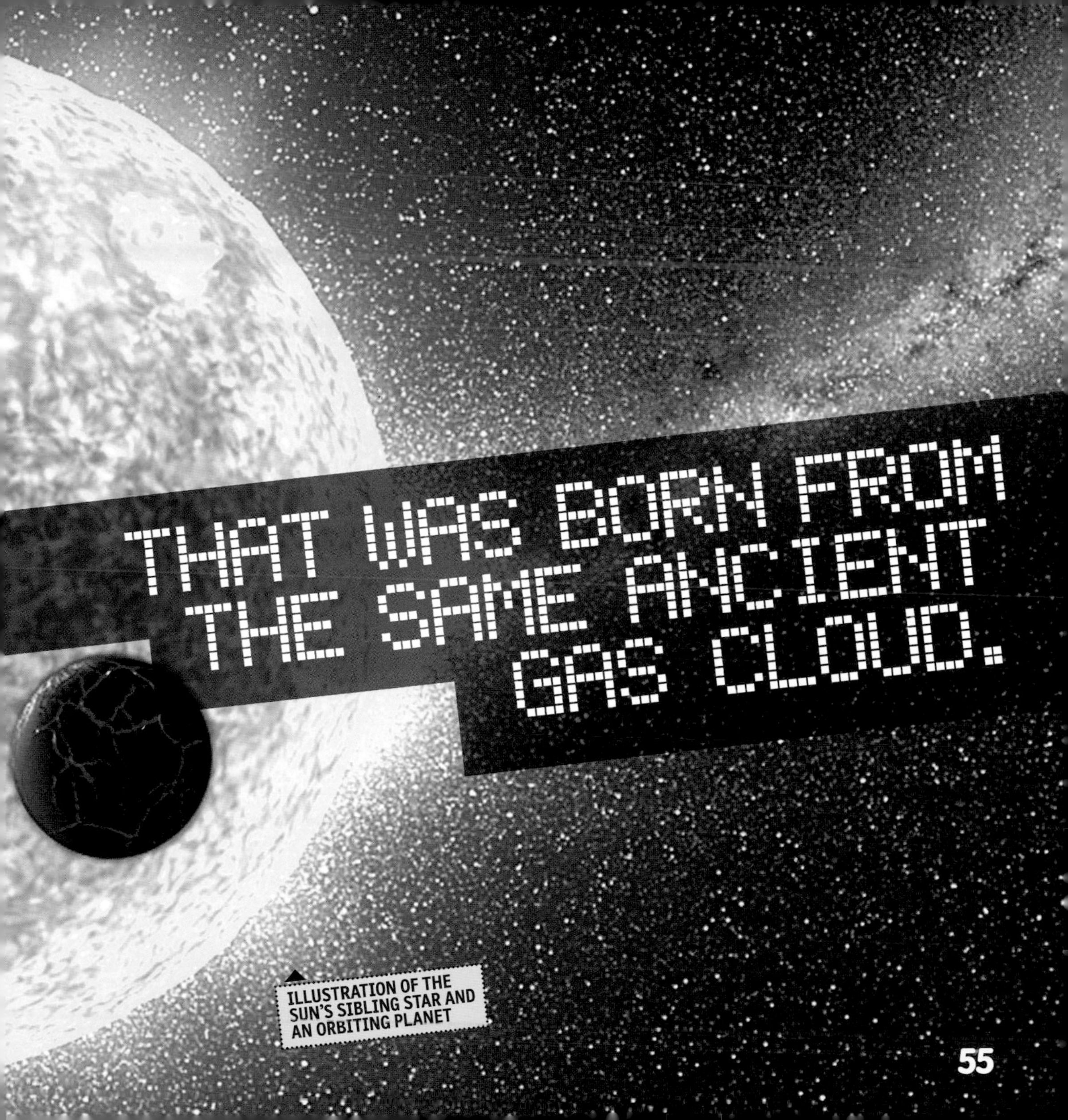

THAT WAS BORN FROM THE SAME ANCIENT GAS CLOUD.

ILLUSTRATION OF THE
SUN'S SIBLING STAR AND
AN ORBITING PLANET

A group of **Twitter** users in Japan once posted **143,199** tweets in **one** second.

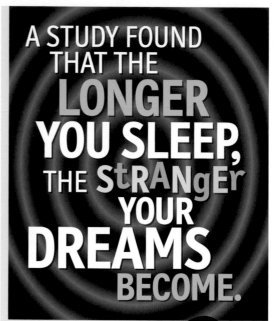

A STUDY FOUND THAT THE **LONGER YOU SLEEP,** THE **StRANgEr** YOUR **DREAMS** BECOME.

VOLCANOES ONCE ERUPTED ON THE **MOON.**

Hello Kitty's full name is Kitty White.

LIFTING WEIGHTS

MAY IMPROVE YOUR

MEMORY.

A FRESHWATER LAKE THE SIZE OF LAKE ONTARIO IS HIDDEN UNDER NEARLY 2.5 MILES OF ICE (4 km) IN ANTARCTICA.

More **American cash** is spent outside the **United States** than inside its borders.

At the **Starbucks** in CIA headquarters, in Virginia, U.S.A., workers aren't allowed to **write** customers' names on **cups.**

THESE PLANTS CAN KILL

THE POISON GARDEN

IN NORTH ENGLAND IS A PUBLIC

GARDEN FILLED WITH DEADLY PLANTS.

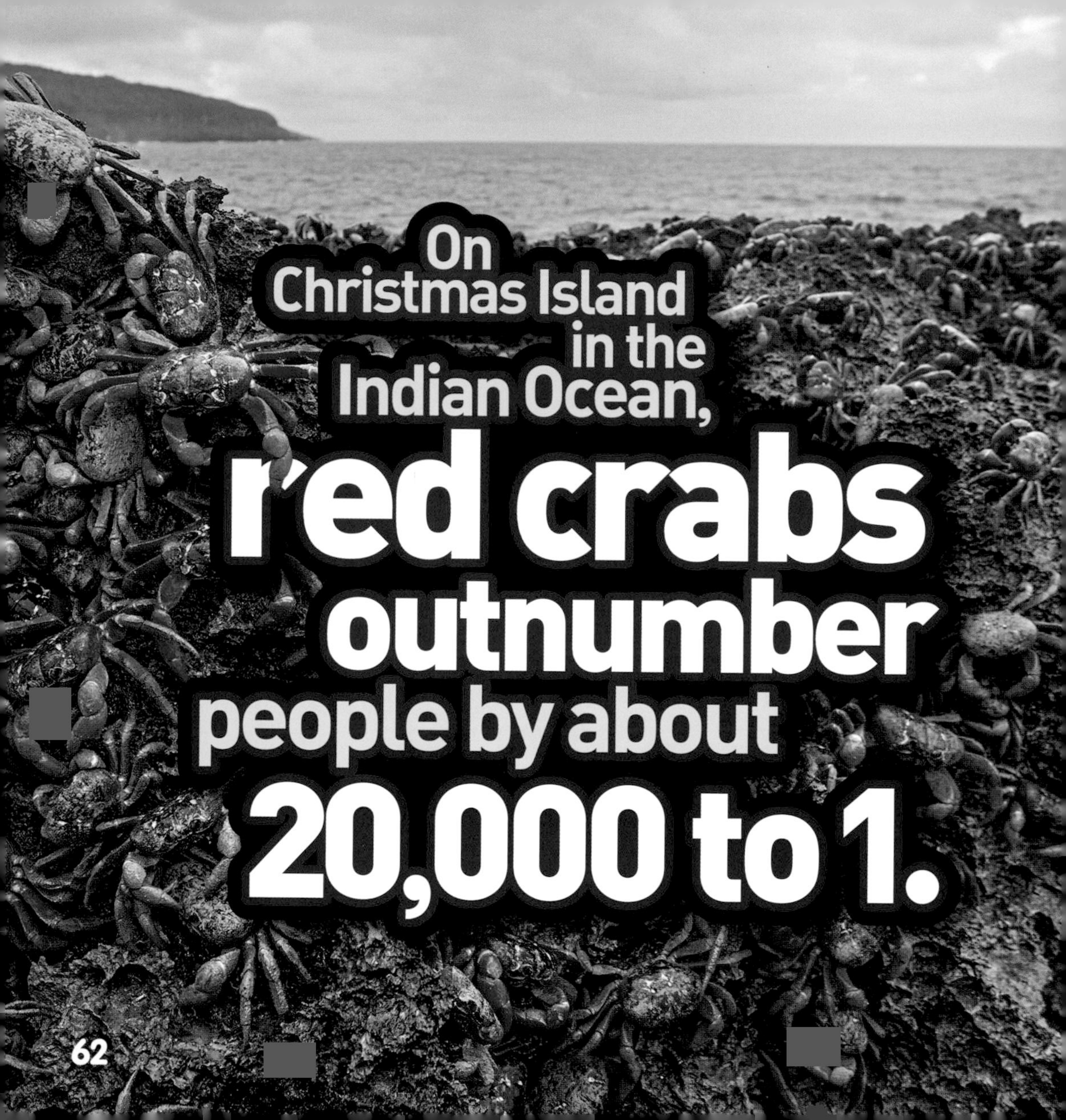

On
Christmas Island
in the
Indian Ocean,

r'ed crabs
outnumber
people by about
20,000 to 1.

FLASHES OF LIGHT SOMETIMES APPEAR IN THE **SKY** BEFORE AND DURING EARTHQUAKES.

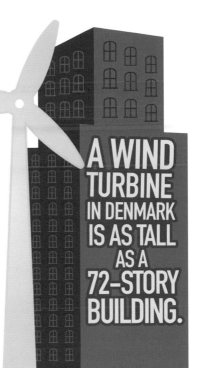

A WIND TURBINE IN DENMARK IS AS TALL AS A 72-STORY BUILDING.

THE ARCHES OF A McDONALD'S IN SEDONA, ARIZONA, U.S.A., ARE TURQUOISE INSTEAD OF YELLOW.

A CHOCOLATE BAR NAMED **CHICKEN DINNER** USED TO BE SOLD IN THE UNITED STATES.

Just a **teaspoon** (5 mL) of a **neutron star's matter** would weigh **six billion tons.** (5.5 billion t)

About **30 million** American adults don't use the **Internet**— more people than the entire population of **Nepal.**

ONE FRENCH ARTIST
CREATES **FACE MASKS** USING
TOILET PAPER ROLLS.

A GROUP OF GOATS

In **Japan,**
you can
buy
doughnuts
stuffed
with
ramen
noodles.

A **POMERANIAN**
BECAME THE **FASTEST DOG**
ON TWO PAWS AFTER
WALKING NEARLY **33 FEET**
IN LESS THAN SEVEN SECONDS (10 m)
ON HIS **HIND LEGS.**

THE U.S. SUPREME COURT BUILDING IN WASHINGTON, D.C., HAS A BASKETBALL COURT ON ITS TOP FLOOR.

NEW YORK CITY'S NEW YEAR'S EVE BALL IS MADE UP OF 2,688 CRYSTAL PANELS.

A STUDY FOUND THAT BABIES BORN IN WINTER TEND TO CRAWL SOONER THAN BABIES BORN IN SUMMER.

A Dutch **artist** created a **69**-foot-long (21-m) **wooden hippo** and floated it down London's River Thames.

A FARMER IN CHINA GROWS PEARS SHAPED LIKE BABIES.

Restaurant diners *who sit by a window tend to order* **salads** *more often, according to one study.*

Osprey birds build nests **big enough** to fit an **adult human inside.**

Walt Disney World's *Cinderella* **Castle**

contains a *hotel suite* that **sleeps** six people.

A company in the Middle East makes bodysuits for camels to wear while training for races.

THE
**AMAZON
RAIN FOREST**
IS ABOUT TWICE
THE SIZE OF
INDIA.

MORE THAN
**100 MILLION
YEARS AGO,**
INDIA WAS AN
ISLAND.

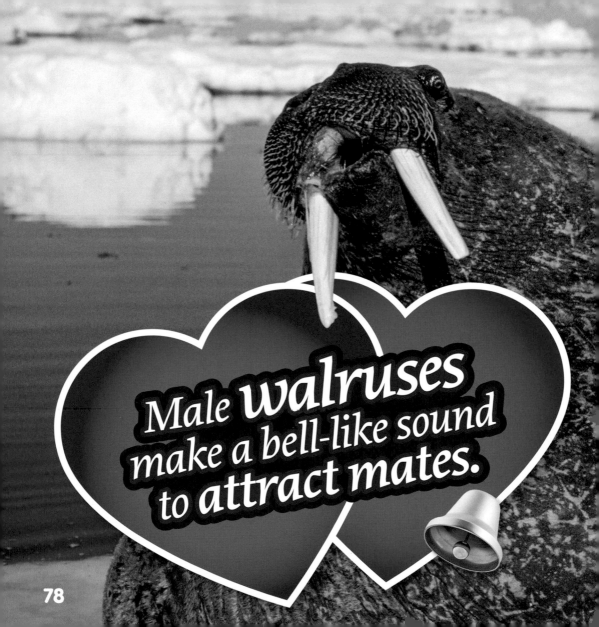

Male **walruses** make a bell-like sound to **attract mates.**

Some **squat lobsters**— a kind of crustacean— are covered in **hairlike bristles.**

A MAN IN ILLINOIS, U.S.A., **BUILT A PICKUP TRUCK** THAT LOOKS AS IF IT HAS BEEN **FLIPPED** UPSIDE DOWN.

ZUCCHINIS ARE ABOUT 95 PERCENT WATER.

YOU'RE 30 TIMES MORE LIKELY TO LAUGH WHEN YOU'RE AROUND FRIENDS THAN WHEN YOU'RE ALONE!

Hagfish digest food through their skin.

Mexico once had **three different presidents** in power in one day.

An **Indian** man set a world record by **drumming** **2,109** drumbeats in one minute.

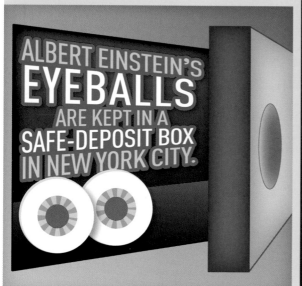

ALBERT EINSTEIN'S **EYEBALLS** ARE KEPT IN A SAFE-DEPOSIT BOX IN NEW YORK CITY.

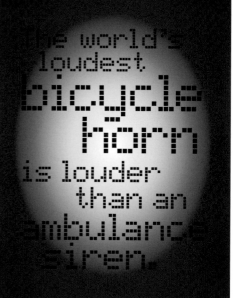

The world's loudest **bicycle horn** is louder than an ambulance siren.

A BEAVER'S IRON-RICH DIET TURNS ITS FRONT TEETH ORANGE.

There are more than **1,000 varieties of mango.**

IN 12TH-CENTURY CHINA, PEOPLE WORE SUNGLASSES WITH LENSES MADE FROM QUARTZ, A TYPE OF CRYSTAL.

83

The biggest X-ray laser in the world **CAN PRODUCE 27,000 LIGHT FLASHES** in one second.

THE REAL-LIFE GLACIER FEATURED IN *STAR WARS: EPISODE V THE EMPIRE STRIKES BACK* AS PLANET **HOTH** COULD DISAPPEAR ENTIRELY BY 2100.

The **BRAINS** of some **SPIDERS** GROW into their **LEGS.**

Some **200 GALLONS** (757 L) of **CREAM SPILLED INTO A SEWER** in Richmond, Virginia, U.S.A.

THIEVES IN ENGLAND STOLE 24,000 BEES FROM A COUNTRY ESTATE.

THE ATLANTIC OCEAN GROWS WIDER BY ABOUT AN INCH (2.5 CM) **EVERY YEAR.**

DINERS at a restaurant in TORONTO, CANADA, eat completely in THE DARK.

DINERS are more likely to order an item if **IT IS LISTED INSIDE A BOX** on the **MENU.**

STUDENTS in ancient Greece **wore necklaces of ROSEMARY** to help them **WITH THEIR EXAMS.**

A SOLAR-ENERGY FARM in Morocco is the size of about **260 FOOTBALL FIELDS.**

The town of **BORING, OREGON, U.S.A.,** is a sister city of the town of **DULL, SCOTLAND.**

The **TERM "ASTRONAUT"** comes from **GREEK** words meaning **"STAR SAILOR."**

That's Weird!

Australia's Great Barrier Reef is roughly the size of Italy.

A crosswalk light in Lisbon, Portugal, featured a figure **dancing to music** as the **stop signal.**

SOME **POLICE CARS** IN DUBAI, UNITED ARAB EMIRATES, CAN GO MORE THAN **220 MILES** (354 km/h) AN HOUR.

THERE ARE
FIVE TIMES
AS MANY
BICYCLES
AS CARS IN
COPENHAGEN,
DENMARK.

IT'S IMPOSSIBLE FOR A **BAT** TO STAND UPRIGHT.

TOGETHER, A
**TARSIER'S
EYES**
WEIGH NEARLY AS
MUCH AS
ITS BRAIN.

As a training tool, the U.S. military created a plan to combat zombies.

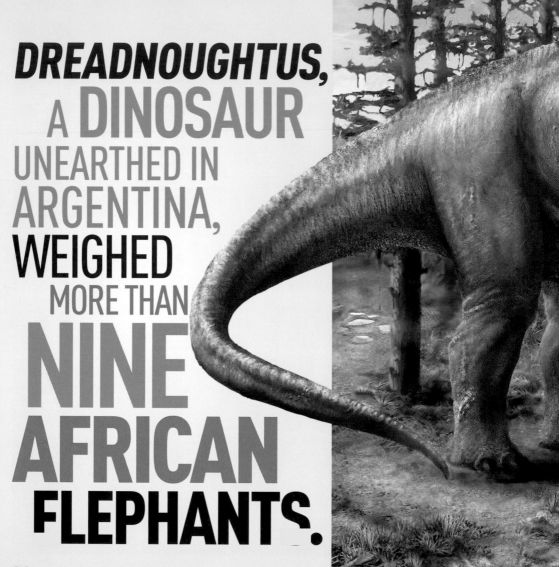

DREADNOUGHTUS, A **DINOSAUR** UNEARTHED IN ARGENTINA, **WEIGHED** MORE THAN **NINE AFRICAN FLEPHANTS.**

By **snapping** its **claw,** the **pistol shrimp** creates a jet of water that can travel **62 miles** (100 km/h) **an hour.**

Roman gladiators consumed an ***energy drink*** containing ash.

Algae sometimes **grow** on **sloth fur.**

SCIENTISTS THINK SOME 20 BILLION PLANETS IN OUR GALAXY COULD SUPPORT ALIEN LIFE.

Buttered **bread** topped with **sprinkles** is a popular **breakfast** in the Netherlands.

SCIENTISTS CREATED A **FORK** THAT MEASURES HOW LONG YOU PAUSE BETWEEN BITES TO SHOW *HOW **FAST** YOU'RE **EATING**.*

SOME KINDS OF **APPLES** **ARE** **PINK** ON THE INSIDE.

In the 1950s, **dyed goat hair** was used for **miniature golf** putting greens.

The first steam **locomotive** made in the United States **lost a race** to a **horse.**

SOME OLD JETS ARE PLACED

IN AIRPLANE GRAVEYARDS.

SCIENTISTS HAVE DETERMINED THAT THE COMET KNOWN AS 67P SMELLS LIKE A MIX OF ROTTEN EGGS, CAT URINE, AND BITTER ALMONDS.

CAMELS ARE BORN WITHOUT HUMPS.

HERMIT CRABS
COMMUNICATE BY CHIRPING.

Some **snakes** can see the **heat** given off by mammals' **bodies.**

BOXER DOGS SOMETIMES FIGHT BY STANDING ON THEIR **HIND LEGS** AND BATTING EACH OTHER WITH THEIR **FRONT PAWS.**

Some **worms** that live on **coral reefs** look like tiny, colorful Christmas trees.

Scientists used a **robot** disguised as a **penguin** to study real **emperor penguins.**

Candidates named Darth Vader and Master Yoda have run for office in Ukraine.

A MAN BUILT **A DRONE** THAT LOOKS LIKE HAN SOLO'S SHIP, THE **MILLENNIUM FALCON.**

IS PARTLY BASED ON TIBETAN AND NEPALI.

IN 1921,

NEARLY

76

(193 cm) INCHES

OF SNOW

FELL IN

24 HOURS

ON SILVER LAKE,
COLORADO, U.S.A.

One
volcano in
Indonesia burns
with **electric blue flames.**

The Super Soaker **water gun** was originally called the **Power Drencher.**

EVERY DAY, **100 TONS OF** (91 t) **COSMIC DUST FROM SPACE** ENTERS EARTH'S ATMOSPHERE— THAT'S THE SAME WEIGHT AS **400 MOUNTAIN GORILLAS.**

HERDS OF **BUFFALO- SIZE** RODENTS ONCE ROAMED SOUTH AMERICA.

HONEYPOT WORKER ANTS,

WHICH STORE NECTAR IN THEIR BODIES, CAN SWELL TO THE SIZE OF A **GRAPE.**

Shoppers are more likely to buy a product if they touch it, one study found.

The name **Crayola** is a combination of two French words that together mean **"oily chalk."**

THE TEETH OF AT LEAST TWO SHARK SPECIES ARE NATURALLY COATED IN FLUORIDE, A MAIN INGREDIENT IN TOOTHPASTE.

IN SAGADA, PHILIPPINES, **COFFINS** *NAILED* TO A CLIFF FACE RATHER THAN **BURIED** UNDERGROUND.

CUCUMBERS WERE KNOWN AS "COWCUMBERS" UNTIL THE MID-19TH CENTURY.

LOUISIANA, U.S.A., IS HOME TO SOME **500,000** WILD PIGS.

A
New York City
artist invented a
waffle iron
that makes
waffles
shaped like a
computer keyboard.

COFFEE WITH CREAM STAYS HOTTER LONGER THAN PLAIN BLACK COFFEE.

AS A HEN GETS OLDER, SHE PRODUCES BIGGER EGGS.

THE INTERNATIONAL SPACE STATION WEIGHS MORE THAN 300 CARS.

A WARM GOLF BALL WILL TRAVEL FARTHER THROUGH THE AIR THAN A COLD ONE.

Every year,
300 million golf balls
are lost or thrown away
in the
United States.

GOLF WAS BANNED IN 15TH-CENTURY SCOTLAND.

ONE KIND OF MITE CAN SPRINT 20 TIMES FASTER THAN A CHEETAH, AS MEASURED IN BODY LENGTHS TRAVELED EACH SECOND.

You can buy "smartshoes" that give directions by **buzzing** your left or right foot to **signal** which way to turn.

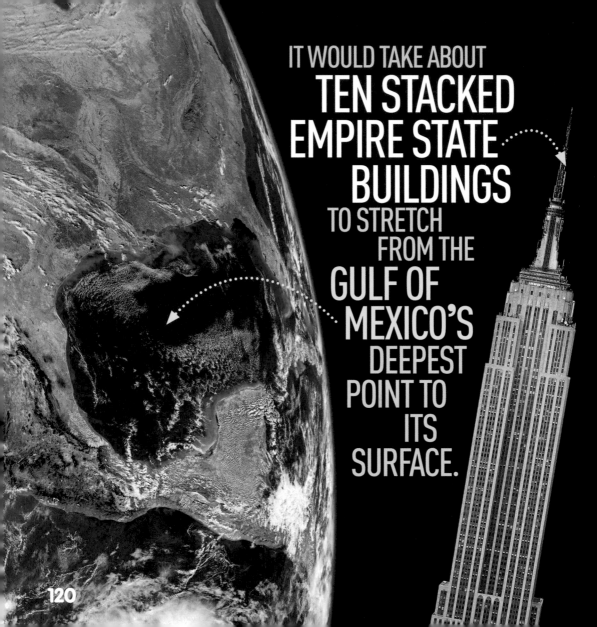

IT WOULD TAKE ABOUT **TEN STACKED EMPIRE STATE BUILDINGS** TO STRETCH FROM THE **GULF OF MEXICO'S** DEEPEST POINT TO ITS SURFACE.

Crocodiles sometimes climb trees.

ONE TYPE OF **OWL** IN AUSTRALIA BARKS LIKE A DOG.

DUST STORMS ON MARS CAN GROW BIGGER THAN THE **CONTINENTAL UNITED STATES.**

One fast-food chain **INVENTED THE FRORK—** a fork to eat **FRENCH FRIES.**

A TEENAGER'S BURIED TREASURE from 1981 was recently DISCOVERED in a VILLAGE in ENGLAND.

More than one million volcanoes are **UNDER EARTH'S OCEAN.**

VISITORS to a park in **SINGAPORE** can sit under trees WHOSE **"LEAVES"** **ARE MADE** OF **UMBRELLAS.**

THE **MOON** TAKES THE SAME NUMBER OF DAYS TO ROTATE AROUND EARTH AS IT DOES TO **SPIN ONCE ON ITS AXIS.**

To help prevent drowning, inventors have created a **NECKLACE** that will **INFLATE** if you stay underwater too long.

DOLPHINS shed their **OUTER LAYER** of skin every **TWO HOURS.**

VOG = TOXIC FOG CREATED BY VOLCANIC ERUPTIONS

A COMPANY ONCE MADE **GUMBALLS** THAT LOOKED LIKE **MEATBALLS**.

A man in France recently discovered he was the **OWNER** of a **"LOST" DRAWING** by **Leonardo da Vinci** valued at **$15.8 MILLION**.

There is **STAR DUST** on city rooftops, sidewalks, and park benches.

IN CHURCHILL, CANADA, there is a **JAIL** for **POLAR BEARS.**

That's Weird!

125

ICE SCULPTORS IN TEXAS, U.S.A., RE-CREATED SCENES FROM *FROSTY THE SNOWMAN* USING **TWO MILLION POUNDS OF ICE.**

Grasshopper Glacier in Montana, U.S.A., contains layers of **grasshoppers** preserved in ice.

Certain **radio signals** coming from **Jupiter** sound like **popcorn popping.**

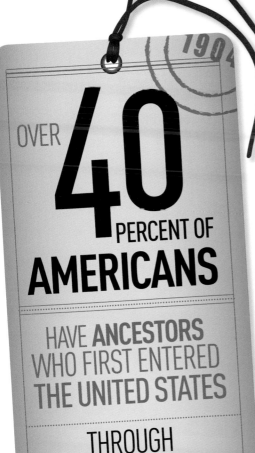

OVER **40** PERCENT OF **AMERICANS**

HAVE **ANCESTORS** WHO FIRST ENTERED **THE UNITED STATES**

THROUGH **ELLIS ISLAND** IN **NEW YORK BAY.**

CURIOUS GEORGE WAS ORIGINALLY NAMED FIFI.

SCIENTISTS LANDED A REMOTE-CONTROLLED SPACECRAFT ON A COMET THAT WAS TRAVELING **84,000 MILES** (135,185 km/h) AN HOUR.

MOUNTAIN LIONS HAVE EXTRA-LARGE **TASTE BUDS** ON THEIR TONGUES THAT HELP SCRAPE **MEAT** FROM BONES.

The **cruise ship** Queen Mary 2 *has a plant that makes* **freshwater** *from* **saltwater.**

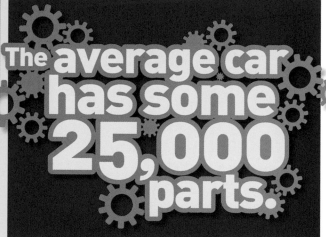

The **average car has some 25,000 parts.**

THE CREATOR OF WONDER WOMAN

ALSO INVENTED AN EARLY VERSION OF THE LIE DETECTOR.

IT TOOK THE INVENTOR OF THE **RUBIK'S CUBE** MORE THAN A **MONTH TO SOLVE THE PUZZLE** AFTER SCRAMBLING IT FOR THE FIRST TIME.

THE **RUBIK'S CUBE** WITH THE MOST SQUARES IS 17-BY-17-BY-17 CUBES.

Some **streets** in Seattle, Washington, U.S.A., **boast** **artwork** that only becomes **visible** when splashed with **water.**

The **DISCO CLAM** uses flashes of light reflected from its lips to ward off predators.

No cars are allowed on **Sark Island** in the **English Channel.**

IF BUNDLED TOGETHER, ALL THE BRANCHES OF A TREE WOULD BE ABOUT AS THICK AS ITS TRUNK.

THE AVERAGE PENCIL HAS ENOUGH GRAPHITE

MOOSE are also called **RUBBER-NOSED** swamp donkeys.

Cashew nuts and poison ivy are closely related.

AFRICA'S NILE RIVER IS LONGER THAN THE

TO DRAW A LINE THAT'S 35 MILES LONG.

(56 km)

The **Tinkerbell wasp** is only **two and a half times** the width of a **human hair.**

WIDTH OF THE CONTIGUOUS **UNITED STATES.**

SWARMS OF JELLYFISH
HAVE APPEARED IN

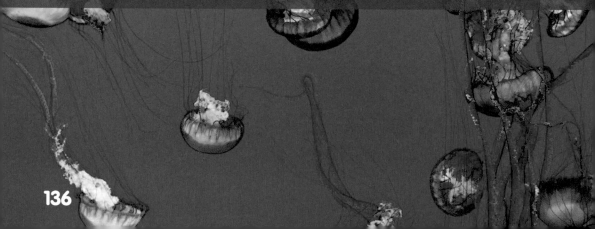

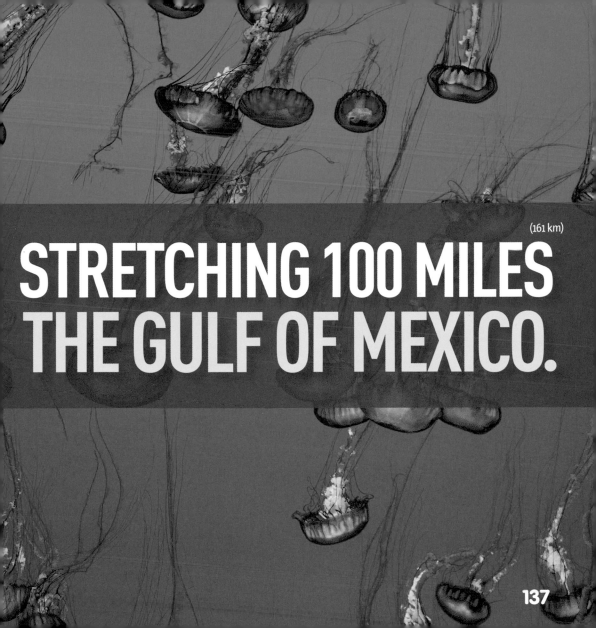

(161 km)

STRETCHING 100 MILES THE GULF OF MEXICO.

THE **DIVING BELL SPIDER** IS THE ONLY SPIDER THAT LIVES ITS **LIFE** ENTIRELY **UNDERWATER.**

THE PLANET KEPLER-413B WOBBLES LIKE A *SPINNING TOP.*

A study found that saying "OW" can help you tolerate pain better.

THE EIFFEL TOWER "GROWS" ABOUT SIX INCHES TALLER IN SUMMER, WHEN THE HEAT MAKES ITS IRON EXPAND.

(15 cm)

SEVERAL **CAVES** IN KENTUCKY, U.S.A., ARE HOME TO A SPECIES OF SEE-THROUGH, **EYELESS SHRIMP.**

Canadians eat more doughnuts than any other country's citizens.

NASA'S HUBBLE TELESCOPE CAPTURED AN IMAGE OF A GALAXY CLUSTER THAT LOOKS LIKE A SMILEY FACE.

THE **POLICE SQUAD** OF ONE SOUTHERN **RUSSIAN TOWN** WAS MADE UP ENTIRELY OF **IDENTICAL TWINS.**

You can **cycle** down a **glow-in-the-dark** **bike path** in the Netherlands.

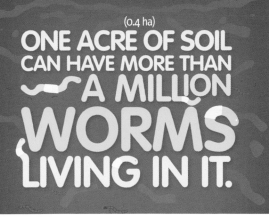

MORE THAN 100 MILES (161 km) OF **MINING TUNNELS** EXIST UNDER DETROIT, MICHIGAN, U.S.A.

(0.4 ha)
ONE ACRE OF SOIL CAN HAVE MORE THAN A MILLION WORMS LIVING IN IT.

Google used a camel *with a* camera mounted on its hump to help map a desert *in the United Arab Emirates.*

SPRAY FROM AFRICA'S VICTORIA FALLS CAN SHOOT 1,600 FEET IN THE AIR.

(500 m)

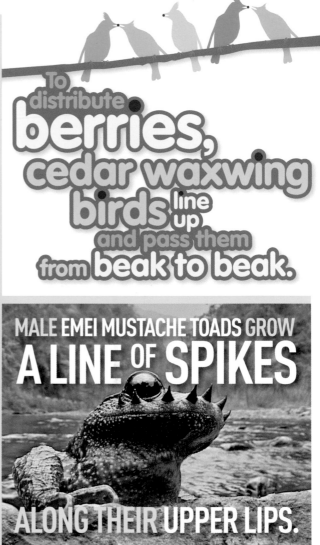

To distribute **berries,** cedar waxwing **birds** line up and pass them from **beak to beak.**

MALE EMEI MUSTACHE TOADS GROW **A LINE OF SPIKES** ALONG THEIR UPPER LIPS.

ANCIENT HAWAIIANS SOMETIMES MADE LEIS OUT OF **BONES.**

EMPEROR **PENGUINS** CAN'T TASTE THE **FISH THEY EAT.**

Inventors used a **3-D printer** to produce a working electric car.

IMTS 2014

MARINE **SNAILS' TEETH** ARE THE **STRONGEST** MATERIAL FOUND IN NATURE.

Caribou release an odor from their **ankles** when threatened.

A more than **500-year-old bed** that may have belonged to **King Henry VII** was recently found in a **parking lot** in England.

About **one-quarter** of the world's **hazelnut** supply is used to make **Nutella.**

You can buy a **guitar pick** made from a **meteorite.**

In the United States, more than **20 million tons** (18 million t) of **salt** are spread on snowy roads, parking lots, sidewalks, and driveways each year.

A double somersault with a **TWIST** performed on a trampoline is called a **fliffis.**

Scientists think that **sperm whales** can detect a **swimmer** more than **one mile** (1.6 km) above them.

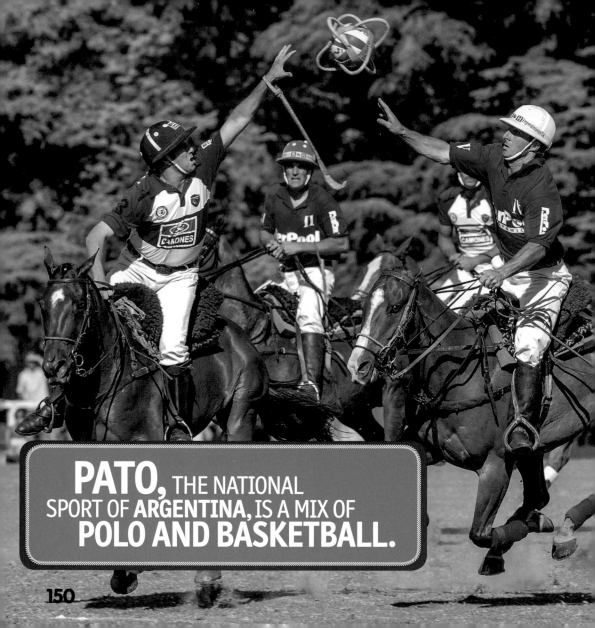

PATO, THE NATIONAL SPORT OF **ARGENTINA,** IS A MIX OF **POLO AND BASKETBALL.**

The average person can recognize about a trillion smells.

The @ symbol is almost five centuries old.

Elizabeth II, Queen of England, served as a mechanic in World War II.

The _Titanic_ was held together by 3 million rivets.

CALIFORNIA INVENTORS CREATED A REAL-LIFE HOVERBOARD.

HENDO

WATCHING FISH SWIM IN AN AQUARIUM CAN REDUCE STRESS, A STUDY FOUND.

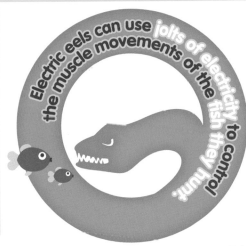

Electric eels can use jolts of electricity to control the muscle movements of the fish they hunt.

YORKSHIRE TERRIER + POODLE

YORKIPOO

THE ISLAND OF MAURITIUS IN THE INDIAN OCEAN HAS MULTICOLORED SAND DUNES.

IN 1808, TWO FRENCHMEN FOUGHT A DUEL WHILE FLOATING IN BALLOONS SOME 2,700 FEET (820 m) ABOVE GROUND.

AMERICAN ASTRONAUTS CAN VOTE IN ELECTIONS FROM SPACE.

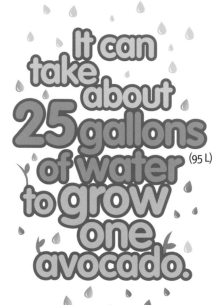

It can take about 25 gallons of water (95 L) to grow one avocado.

The noises **Tasmanian devils** make when eating can be heard **a mile away.** (1.6 km)

THE DESERT-DWELLING **FENNEC FOX** HAS HAIRY FOOTPADS THAT PROTECT ITS FEET FROM HOT SAND.

U.S. FAMILIES SPEND AN ESTIMATED **$9 BILLION** ON BACK-TO-SCHOOL **CLOTHES.**

President Gerald Ford once worked as a park ranger.

THAT'S FIN-TASTIC!

A GROUP OF SHARKS

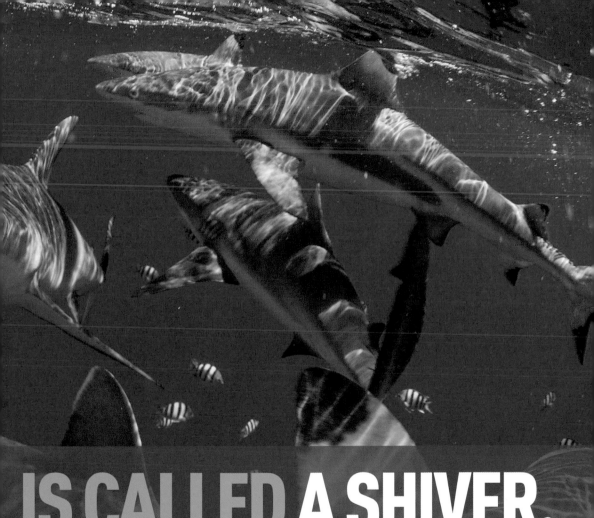

IS CALLED A SHIVER.

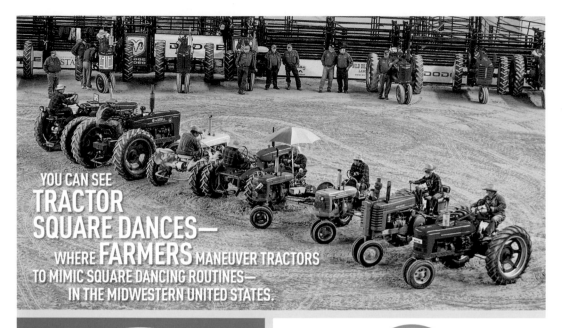

YOU CAN SEE **TRACTOR SQUARE DANCES**— WHERE **FARMERS** MANEUVER TRACTORS TO MIMIC SQUARE DANCING ROUTINES— IN THE MIDWESTERN UNITED STATES.

PEOPLE WHO ARE FREQUENTLY **HUGGED** EXPERIENCE **LESS SEVERE COLD** SYMPTOMS, A STUDY FOUND.

Someone who plays **marbles** is called a **mibster**.

A HAMSTER'S CHEEK POUCHES EXTEND ALL THE WAY TO ITS hips.

SOME BOWHEAD WHALES LIVE FOR MORE THAN 200 YEARS.

LAZE = MISTY CLOUDS THAT FORM WHEN HOT LAVA ENTERS THE OCEAN

A study found that the **TEMPERATURE INSIDE OUR CELLS** can reach **122°F** (50°C).

An Italian artist designed a **BATHTUB** shaped like a **HIGH-HEELED SHOE.**

A **TREE** in **CHILE** is called the **MONKEY PUZZLE TREE—** even though **NO MONKEYS** live in the area.

TWO-THIRDS OF AMERICANS use their **FEET** to **FLUSH** PUBLIC **TOILETS,** according to a survey.

ARCHAEOLOGISTS found a **4,000-year-old "FUNERAL GARDEN"** in Luxor, Egypt, where people may have grown **PLANTS MEANT FOR THE AFTERLIFE.**

AN ARGENTINE ARTIST opened an ART GALLERY at 14,000 feet (4,300 m) in the **ANDES MOUNTAINS.**

BRIDES who get married in Orlando, Florida, U.S.A., can ride to their wedding in **CINDERELLA'S** GLASS COACH.

A CHINESE NEWSPAPER was once **printed on paper** made with **500 GRAMS OF GOLD.** (EACH COPY was PRICED at about **$8,100.**)

A VOLCANIC ERUPTION in 1980 caused STREETLIGHTS in some Washington State, U.S.A., cities TO TURN ON IN THE MIDDLE OF THE DAY.

JAPANESE RESEARCHERS created a material out of gel and fabric that is five times **stronger than carbon steel.**

That's Weird!

MORE THAN **3,000** YEARS AGO, DECORATED **OSTRICH EGGS WERE TRADED AS LUXURY ITEMS** IN THE **MIDDLE EAST.**

APPLES CAN RIPEN TEN TIMES FASTER AT ROOM TEMPERATURE THAN IN THE REFRIGERATOR.

AT AN OPERA HOUSE ON THE U.S.–CANADIAN BORDER, THE STAGE IS IN CANADA WHILE MOST SEATS ARE IN THE UNITED STATES.

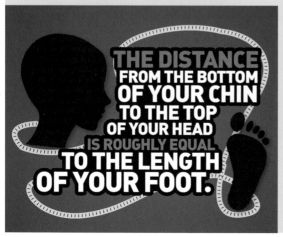

THE DISTANCE FROM THE BOTTOM OF YOUR CHIN TO THE TOP OF YOUR HEAD IS ROUGHLY EQUAL TO THE LENGTH OF YOUR FOOT.

One **rock** in Joshua Tree National Park in California, U.S.A., resembles a giant human skull.

A MALE RED DEER'S ANTLERS CAN GROW

TO A WEIGHT OF 60 POUNDS (27 kg) IN THREE MONTHS.

Six of the **seven dwarfs** in the 1937 animated movie *Snow White and the Seven Dwarfs* have eyebrows modeled after Walt Disney's.

Temperatures on Mercury can drop more than 1000°F (550°C) in one day.

A PENNY ISSUED BY THE U.S. MINT IN 1793 SOLD AT AUCTION FOR $2.3 MILLION.

The first baseball caps were made from straw.

The most **commonly used noun** in the English **language is** " **people.**"

Pelicans can hold more food in their beaks than in their stomachs.

Extreme athletes **have skied** *from the summit of Mount Everest to a base camp* 12,000 *feet below.*

(3,660 m)

ONE **ARTIST** PAINTED A PICTURE OF BASKETBALL PLAYER **YAO MING,** USING A **BASKETBALL** AS A **"PAINTBRUSH."**

Laid end to end, New York City's subway tracks would stretch from the Big Apple to Chicago, Illinois, U.S.A.

YOU CAN FIND OVER

2,000
ROCK
ARCHES
IN **ARCHES**
NATIONAL PARK,

IN UTAH, U.S.A.

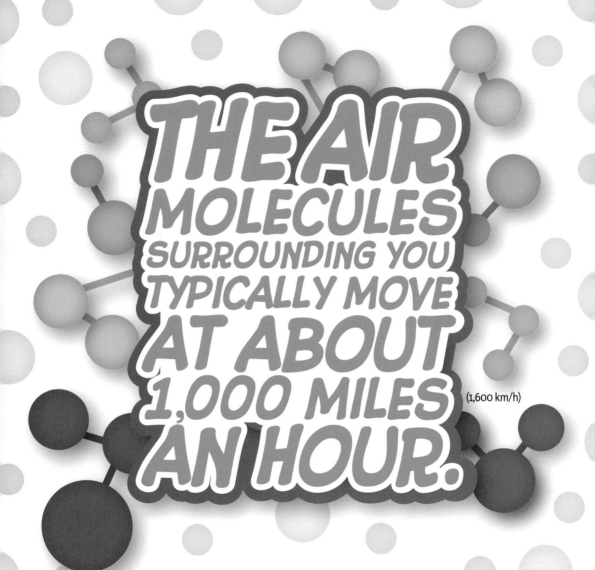

THE AIR MOLECULES SURROUNDING YOU TYPICALLY MOVE AT ABOUT 1,000 MILES AN HOUR.

(1,600 km/h)

BOTTLENOSE DOLPHINS SWALLOW THEIR **FOOD WHOLE.**

IN JAPAN, KFC GAVE AWAY **iPHONE CASES SHAPED LIKE GIANT CHICKEN DRUMSTICKS.**

An average of **2.4 million** GO GLE searches happen every minute.

The belly button–like formation on a **navel orange** is where another orange is starting to grow.

PARROTS DON'T HAVE VOCAL CORDS.

A newborn **sea otter's** extra-thick **fur** traps in so much air that it's **impossible** for the animal to **sink.**

SOME **SOCCER BALLS** HAVE A BUILT-IN **CHIP** THAT SIGNALS REFEREES WHEN THE BALL PASSES THE **GOAL LINE.**

3,240 SOCCER BALLS WERE USED DURING THE 2014 WORLD CUP.

PROFESSIONAL **SOCCER PLAYERS** RUN AN AVERAGE OF **SEVEN MILES** DURING EACH (11 km) **GAME.**

AN **INDOOR SOCCER MATCH** IN ALBERTA, CANADA, LASTED **30 HOURS AND 10 MINUTES.**

AN
ATLANTIC PUFFIN
CAN HOLD
AS MANY AS
A DOZEN
SMALL FISH
IN ITS BILL
AT ONE
TIME.

SOME MOTHS
DON'T HAVE
MOUTHS.

183

A BILLBOARD IN RIYADH, SAUDI ARABIA, STRETCHES

Pippi Longstocking's full name is Pippilotta Delicatessa Windowshade Mackrelmint Ephraim's Daughter Longstocking.

Watermelon **seeds** *were found in* **King Tut's tomb.**

Oklahoma, U.S.A., was once hit by **15** TORNADOES in one day.

AN
ARTiST
IN LONDON,
ENGLAND,
CONSTRUCTED A
BUiLDiNG
THAT APPEARS
TO
LEViTATE.

A HEDGEHOG HAS ABOUT

6,000 QUILLS.

Polar bears sometimes communicate by touching noses.

SOME PEOPLE **LACK** THE GENE THAT CAUSES **SMELLY** UNDERARMS.

ONIONS AND **GARLIC** CAN BE USED TO HELP SOAK UP TOXIC SPILLS.

TRISKAIDEKAPHOBIA IS THE FEAR OF THE NUMBER 13.

THE WORLD'S LARGEST DISCO BALL IS MORE THAN 33 FEET (10 m) **IN DIAMETER. ALMOST AS WIDE AS A TENNIS COURT.**

The common **octopus** is the **size of a flea** at birth.

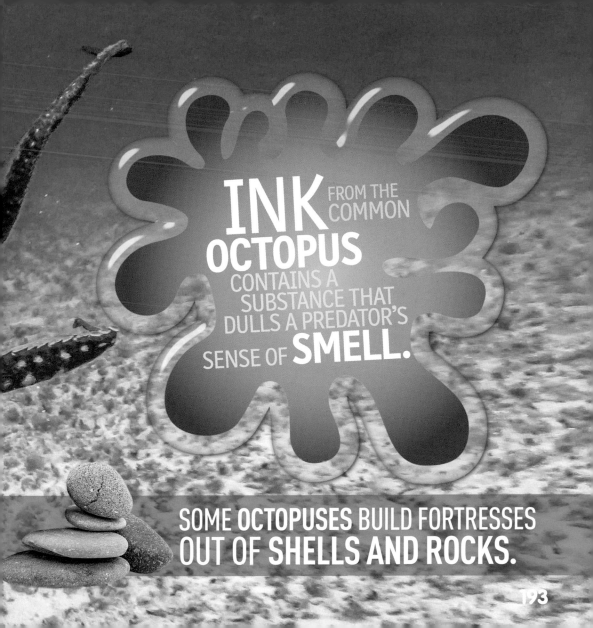

INK FROM THE COMMON **OCTOPUS** CONTAINS A SUBSTANCE THAT DULLS A PREDATOR'S SENSE OF **SMELL.**

SOME **OCTOPUSES** BUILD FORTRESSES OUT OF **SHELLS AND ROCKS.**

A candy company once made Thanksgiving-themed **gumballs** with flavors such as cranberry, turkey, and pumpkin pie.

SOME **21,000** YEARS AGO, MASSIVE **ICEBERGS** FLOATED OFF THE COAST OF FLORIDA, U.S.A.

Scientists have figured out a way to convert **sugar** into **fuel.**

India sent a spacecraft known as **MOM** to Mars.

Researchers are trying to develop a car tire made from dandelions.

MOST SHARKS WOULD SINK IN FRESHWATER.

More than 1,400 varieties of cheese exist in the world.

CERTAIN FERNS EJECT THEIR SPORES WITH A CATAPULT MOTION.

In some large U.S. cities, more than **$2 million** worth of **gold** and **silver** ends up in the sewer systems each year.

A GROUP OF GIRAFFES

A West Indian manatee's **lungs** are two-thirds the length of its body.

Your glabella is the area of skin between your eyebrows.

IN 2014,
TWO PROFESSORS
LIVED FOR

73 DAYS
IN AN

AIRTIGHT
LODGE

ABOUT

25 FEET (7.6 m)

UNDERWATER

OFF THE COAST OF
FLORIDA, U.S.A.

All of
Earth's
land
could fit
in the
Pacific
Ocean.

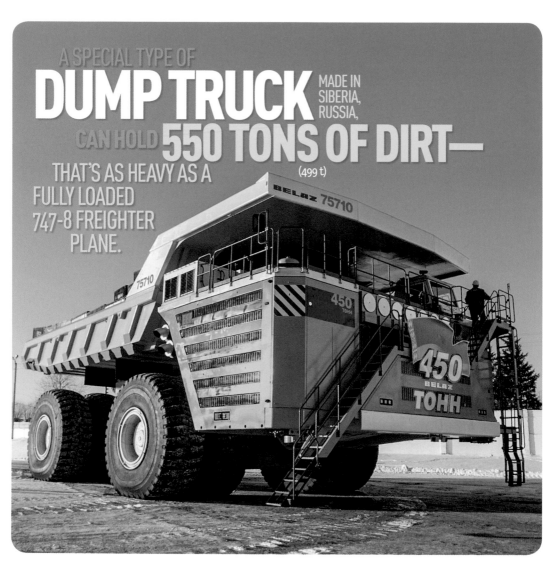

A SPECIAL TYPE OF **DUMP TRUCK** MADE IN SIBERIA, RUSSIA, CAN HOLD **550 TONS OF DIRT—** (499 t) THAT'S AS HEAVY AS A FULLY LOADED 747-8 FREIGHTER PLANE.

The American **goldfinch** sometimes sounds as if it's saying **"po-tay-toe-chip"** when it chirps.

WAVES OFF THE COAST OF PUERTO MALABRIGO, PERU, CAN STRETCH MORE THAN A **MILE LONG.**
(1.6 km)

A SINGLE BANANA IS CALLED A FINGER; A BUNCH IS CALLED **A HAND.**

MALE **KANGAROOS**
FLEX THEIR
BICEPS
TO **IMPRESS** FEMALES.

ENOUGH **CANDY CORN** IS MADE EVERY YEAR TO GIVE EVERY PERSON ON EARTH ONE KERNEL.

89 PERCENT OF PEOPLE EAT A CHOCOLATE

GUESS WHAT?

A rainbow that happens at night isn't called a rainbow! **HMM?**

Maybe you should be more scared of pigs than sharks! **WHY?**

If you wash dishes by hand, you might sneeze less! **WHY?**

WANNA FIND OUT?

The FUN doesn't have to end here! Find these far-out facts and more in *Weird But True! 8.*

NATIONAL GEOGRAPHIC KiDS

weird but true! 8

350 OUTRAGEOUS FACTS

That's Weird!

NATIONAL GEOGRAPHIC KiDS

FACTFINDER

Boldface indicates illustrations.

FACTFINDER

FACTFINDER

PHOTO CREDITS

Published by National Geographic Partners, LLC.
All rights reserved. Reproduction of the whole
or any part of the contents without written
permission from the publisher is prohibited.

Since 1888, the National Geographic Society
has funded more than 12,000 research, explo-
ration, and preservation projects around the
world. The Society receives funds from National
Geographic Partners, LLC, funded in part by
your purchase. A portion of the proceeds from
this book supports this vital work. To learn
more, visit natgeo.com/info.

For more information, visit nationalgeographic
.com, call 1-877-873-6846, or write to the
following address:
National Geographic Partners
1145 17th Street N.W.
Washington, D.C. 20036-4688 U.S.A.

Visit us online at nationalgeographic.com/books

For librarians and teachers:
ngchildrensbooks.org

More for kids from National Geographic:
natgeokids.com

For information about special discounts
for bulk purchases, please contact National
Geographic Books Special Sales:
specialsales@natgeo.com

For rights or permissions inquiries, please
contact National Geographic Books Subsidiary
Rights: bookrights@natgeo.com

Designed by Rachel Hamm Plett, Moduza Design

First edition published 2015
Reissued and updated 2018

Trade paperback ISBN: 978-1-4263-3116-9
Reinforced library binding ISBN:
978-1-4263-3117-6

The publisher would like to thank Jen Agresta,
project manager; Michelle Harris, researcher;
Andrea Silen, project editor; Paige Towler,
project editor; Julide Dengel, art director;
Kathryn Robbins, art director; Ruthie
Thompson, designer; Lori Epstein, photo
director; Hillary Leo, photo editor; Joan
Gossett, production editor; Gus Tello and
Anne LeongSon, production assistants.

Printed in China
22/PPS/4(SC)
22/PPS/2(RLB)